WHAT

Is the little man computer?

Om KIDZ
An imprint of Om Books International

Contents

- What is a computer? 3
- What all can I do with a computer? 3
- What makes a computer work so fast? 4
- What is a supercomputer? 4
- What did the first computer look like? 5
- What were the first computers used for? 5
- What are the different types of computers? 6
- What is a tablet PC? 6
- What is the Little Man Computer? 7
- What was the first portable computer? 7
- What is hardware? 8
- What is software? 8
- What are the main parts of a computer? 9
- What is a keyboard used for? 9
- What is the total number of keys on a keyboard? 10
- What is a QWERTY keyboard? 10
- What does the CPU do for a computer? 11
- What is a computer memory? 11
- What does a computer mouse do? 12
- What did the first computer mouse look like? 12
- What is a USB port? 13
- What is a pen drive? 13
- What is a desktop? 14
- What is an icon? 14
- What is a computer virus? 15
- What can I do to protect my computer from virus? 15
- Index 16

What is a computer?

A computer is an electronic device that receives information or data from us. It can store and process this information by performing calculations and operations on it. The term **computer** is derived from the Latin word '**Computare**' which means 'to compute'.

Find out

What were computers called in the 1950s?

Pocket fact

The word "computer" was first recorded in 1613. It was used to refer to a person who carried out calculations or computations.

What can we do using a computer?

A lot many things! Different people use computers for different purposes. We can use a computer to type documents, send email, play games and browse the Web. Architects, engineers, jewellers and filmmakers—all use computers to design things. Scientists, writers and teachers use computers for research. Businessmen can use computers for general record keeping. The use of computers has made many tasks easy and quick!

What makes a computer work so fast?

The processor! A computer is said to be faster and more efficient when it can carry out maximum number of instructions every second. The overall speed of a computer is managed by the Central Processing Unit (CPU). The processors today are capable of processing over 100 billion instructions per second!

Pocket fact

The Central Processing Unit is also known as the brain of the computer. It sends signals to control the other parts of the computer, almost like how the brain controls our body!

Find out

When was the first supercomputer made?

What is a supercomputer?

A very fast computer! A supercomputer has great speed and memory. It can work thousand times faster than any other computer of its generation. A supercomputer can do arithmetic calculations very fast, so it is used in advanced scientific applications, weather forecasting, and other tasks that need many calculations.

What did the first electronic computer look like?

It was the size of a room! The first electronic computer was called ENIAC- Electronic Numerical Integrator and Computer. It was built by the United States in 1945. ENIAC weighed 30 tons and used 200 kilowatts of electric power.

Pocket fact

ENIAC was no longer in use after 2 October 1955. Only about 10 panels of the 40 exist now.

Find out

Who designed the ENIAC?

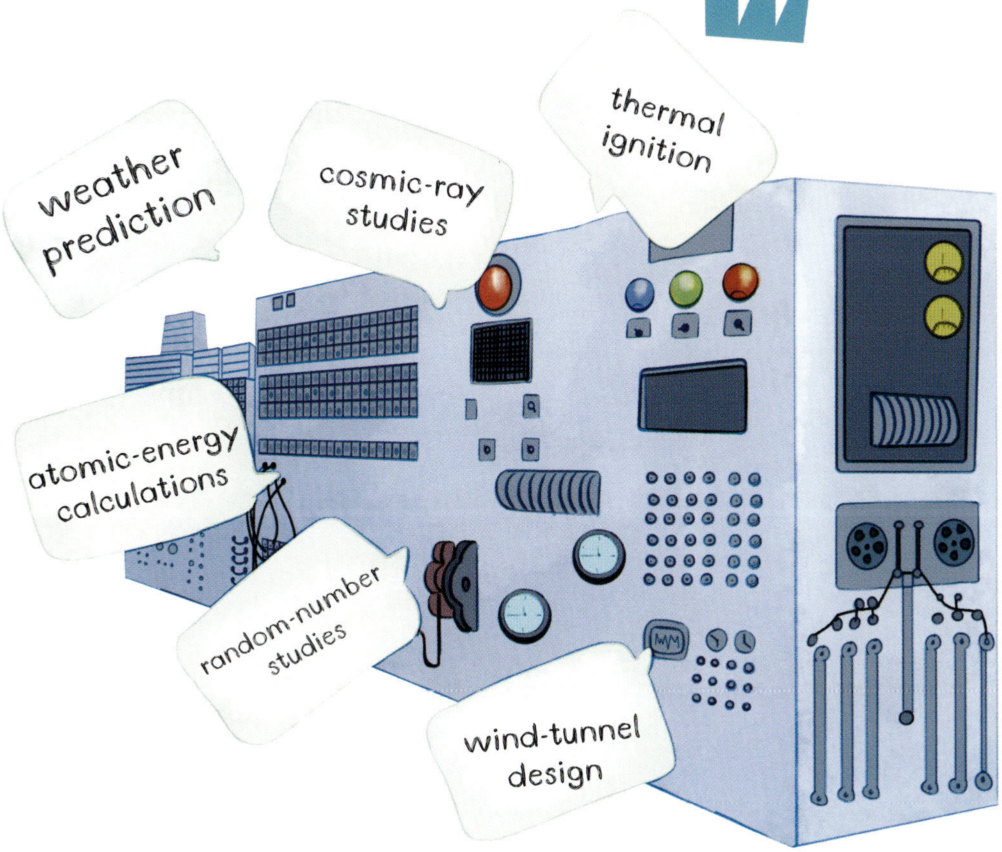

What was the first computer used for?

The uses of the first computer ENIAC included weather prediction, atomic-energy calculations, cosmic-ray studies, thermal ignition, random-number studies and wind-tunnel design. It was also used for other scientific purposes.

What are the different types of computers?

Desktops, laptops and more! Computers come in many shapes and sizes, and they perform many different functions in our daily lives. The different types of computers are *personal computer*, *workstation*, *minicomputer*, *mainframe* and *supercomputer*. Desktop, laptop, notebook and palmtop are some kinds of personal computers.

Find out

What is a stylus?

Pocket fact

The GriDPad!

The GRiDPad was one of the earliest tablets produced in 1989. It had a touch screen and a wired stylus; and weighed just under 5 pounds.

What is a tablet PC?

A Tablet PC or tablet is a small portable computer that is usually smaller than a laptop. It doesn't have a keyboard or a mouse instead has a touch-sensitive screen for typing and navigation. You can do many of the same things using a tablet like that of a desktop– browse the Internet, use apps and also display HD videos.

What is the Little Man Computer?

The Little Man Computer (LMC) is an instructional model of a computer, created by Dr. Stuart Madnick in 1965. The LMC is generally used to teach students, because it models a simple von Neumann architecture computer—which has all the basic features of a modern computer.

Pocket fact

In a laptop, a touch pad can be used in place of an external mouse. It helps you to move the cursor with your finger.

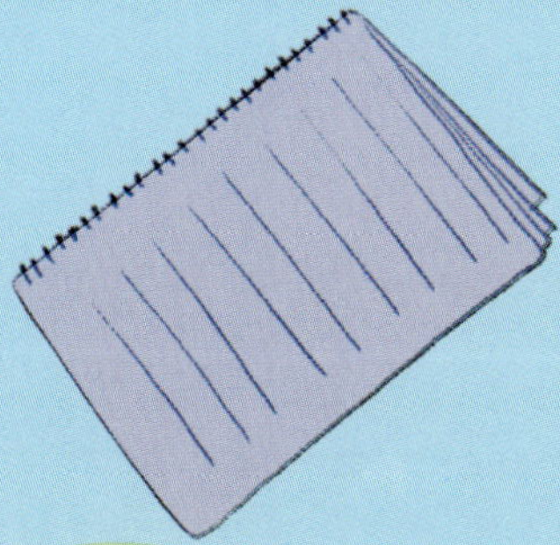

Find out

What is a computer notebook?

What was the first portable computer?

The first truly portable computer was the Osborne 1 developed by Adam Osborne. It was released in April 1981 by the Osborne Computer Corporation. The Osborne 1 was quite different from the modern laptop. It weighed 24.5 pounds and had a 5-inch display.

What is hardware?

Any part of your computer that you can see and touch! Computer hardware refers to the physical parts of a computer, such as the monitor, keyboard, mouse, speakers and CPU. It also includes all of the computer's internal parts.

Find out

Who was Ada Lovelace?

Pocket fact

Z1!

The first computer was called Z1. It was invented by Konrad Zuse in 1936. It had many parts like that of a modern computer—control unit, memory and input-output devices.

What is software?

A set of instructions that tells the computer what and how to do! Software helps us to interact with a computer, its hardware, and perform tasks. Web browsers, games, and apps are examples of software. Without software, most computers would not be able to perform.

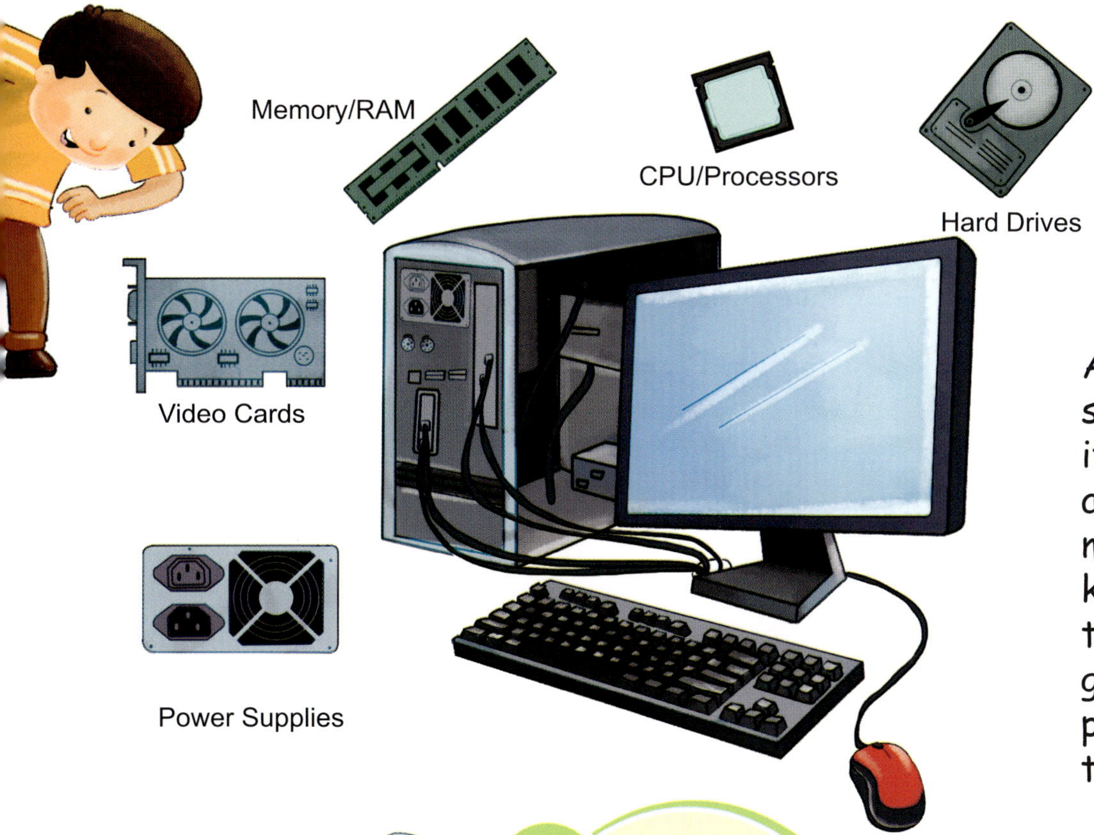

What are the main parts of a computer?

A computer generally consists of several different parts that help it function. But the main parts of a desktop computer include the monitor, the system unit, and the keyboard. The system unit contains the hard drive, disc drive, CPU, graphics card, sound card, and many ports that connect external devices to your computer.

Find out

Which is the longest key on the keyboard?

Pocket fact

The modern computer keyboard was inspired from the invention of the typewriter in 1868. It was Christopher Latham Sholes who invented the QWERTY keyboard that we commonly use today.

What is a keyboard used for?

To communicate with the computer! The keyboard is an input device that is used to enter text. It lets us enter characters and functions into the computer by pressing buttons, or keys. Without the keyboard, it is impossible to type or enter text into the computer!

What is the total number of keys on a keyboard?

It varies from one kind to another! A computer keyboard usually has 101 to 104 keys. These are Alphabet keys, Number keys, Function keys, Arrow keys, Symbol Keys and Special keys. A computer keyboard is quite similar to a typewriter.

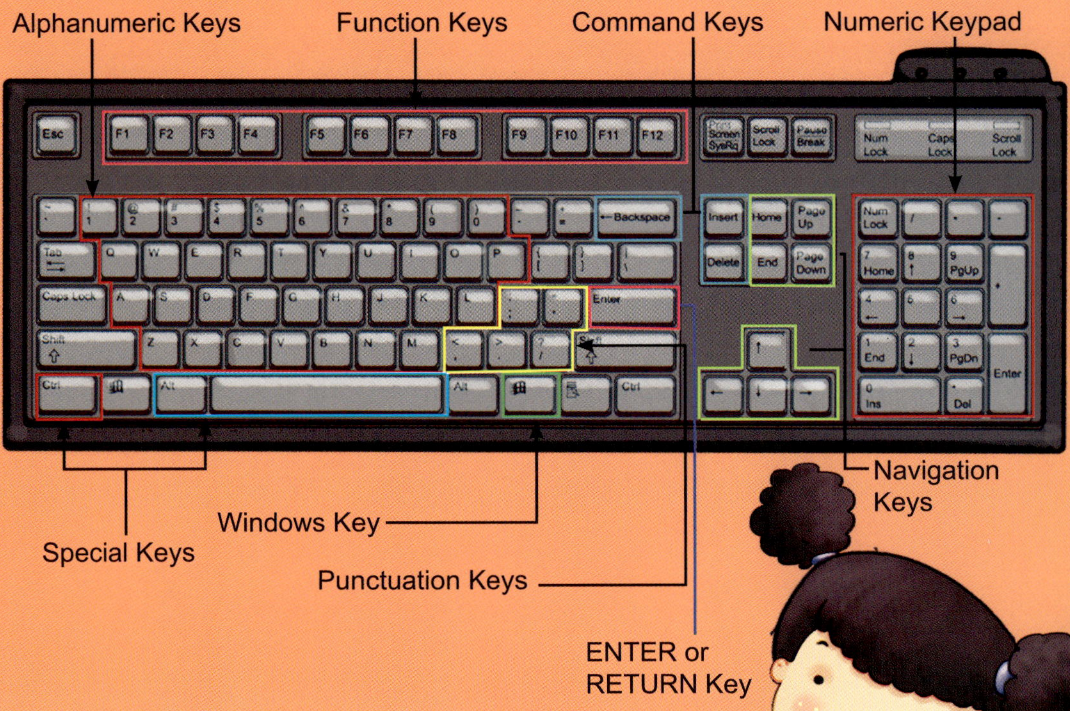

Pocket fact

The French Version!
The AZERTY Keyboard is the French version of the standard QWERTY keyboard. In such a keyboard the Q and W keys have been interchanged with the A and Z keys.

Try this

Find the keys that spell the letters of your name. In which row are they placed on the keyboard?

What is a QWERTY keyboard?

The QWERTY keyboard is the most widely used keyboard layout. It is named so because the sequence of the first six letters from the top left of the keyboard is QWERTY.

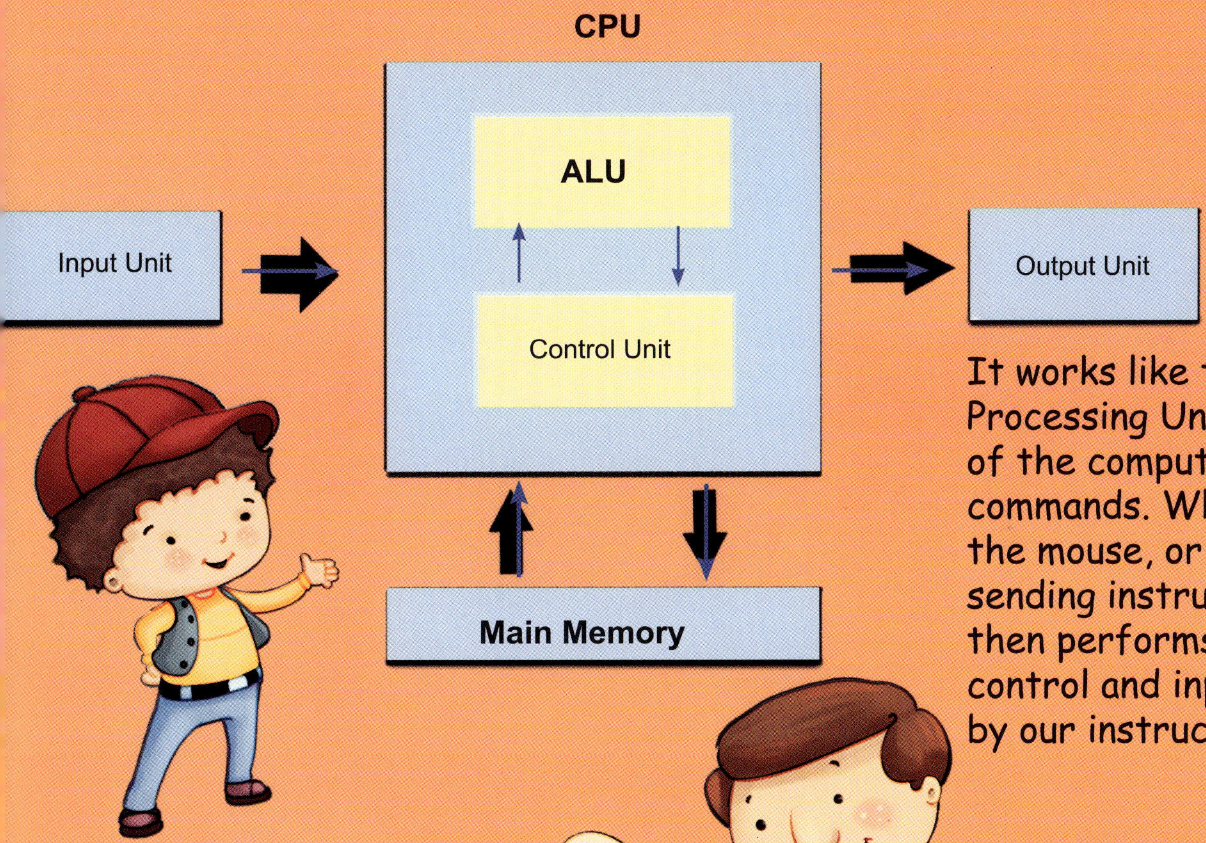

What does the CPU do for a computer?

It works like the brain! CPU i.e. the Central Processing Unit is often called the brain of the computer. Its job is to carry out commands. Whenever you press a key, click the mouse, or start an application, you're sending instructions to the CPU. The CPU then performs the arithmetic, logical, control and input/output operations specified by our instructions and gives us results.

Pocket fact

Bits and Bytes!
A bit is the smallest unit of computer's memory. A set of 8 bits is called a Byte.

Find out

What is clock rate?

What is a computer memory?

A device that stores data or instructions! A computer memory is a space inside the computer where data is stored. It is divided into a large number of small parts called cells. Each cell has a unique address, which varies from zero to memory size minus one. A computer memory is of two types—primary and secondary.

What does a computer mouse do?

It is a pointing device! A mouse is a cursor-control device that has a small palm size box with a round ball at its base. This ball senses the movement of the mouse and sends signals to the CPU when the mouse buttons are pressed. It is used to control the position of the cursor on the screen, but it cannot be used to enter text into the computer.

Pocket fact

The Mouse Wheel
The modern desktop computer mouse also usually includes a mouse wheel that allows you to scroll up and down on a page.

Try this

Can you name the parts of a computer mouse? Give it a try.

What did the first computer mouse look like?

It was much larger than today's mouse! The first computer mouse was invented by a U.S. engineer Douglas Engelbart in the early 1960s. It was made of wood, rectangular in shape, and had a small button on the top right corner. Its wooden base also had two wheels to roll back and forth.

What is a desktop?

The desktop is the area of a computer screen where we see images, windows, icons and other graphical items. Some of the most common icons on the desktop are My Computer, Recycle Bin, Internet browser and My Documents.

Find out

Which alphabet key should you press with the Windows key to get to the desktop?

Pocket fact

The first computer that used a monitor was the Alto. Before that computers made use of television screens as monitors.

What is the START button on the desktop used for?

To help you use programs on the computer! The Start button is found at the bottom left part of a desktop screen. When you click the Start button, the Start Menu opens and you can access all the programs installed on your computer. It acts like a window to enter your computer.

What is a USB port?

A USB port is a small port that allows different devices to be connected to a computer. Some examples of devices that connect to a USB port are printers, keyboards, computer mice, MP3 players and external hard drives. A desktop computer usually has two to four ports in the front and two to eight ports at the back.

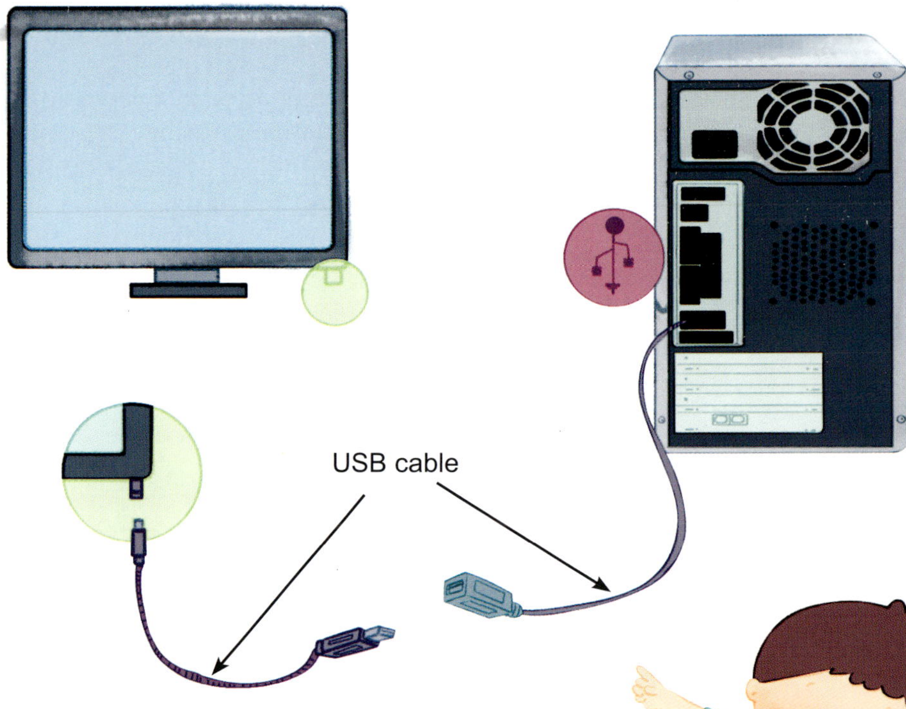

Find out

What are the other names of a pen drive?

Pocket fact

We invented it!
Pen drives were first invented at M-Systems, an Israeli company, in April 1999 by Amir Ban, Dov Moran and Oron Ogdan.

What is a pen drive?

A memory and data transfer device! A pen drive is a device used for storing and transferring audio, video and data files from one computer to another. It is often the size of our thumb and is also called a thumb drive. It connects to a computer through a USB port. Pen drives are available in sizes ranging from 2 GB to 1 TB.

What is a computer virus?

Something that makes our computer sick! A computer virus is a program or script that can cause damage to a computer by stealing information, modifying data, sending e-mail and displaying messages. When the virus is executed, it spreads in the computer by copying itself into or over the files in our computer and affects its working just like a virus makes us sick!

Find out

Which was the first antivirus program?

Pocket fact

The Creeper virus is usually recognised as the first computer virus. It was first detected on ARPANET—a network that was used before the Internet, in the early 1970s.

What can I do to protect my computer from virus?

By using an antivirus! An antivirus is a software program designed to protect your computer from computer viruses. When the antivirus detects a virus, it displays a warning asking what action should be performed. It often displays the options to remove, ignore, or move the file to the vault.

Index

A, B, C
action
arrangement
bits
brain
cell
character
clock rate
command
creeper virus

D, E
design
efficient
engineer
enter
external

I, M
internal
invention
laptop
logical
model

P, S
palmtop
pen Drive
port
prediction
pressing
primary
processor
protect
script
scroll
secondary
space
store
stylus
supercomputer
symbol

T, W
text
thumb Drive
transfer Device
typing
typwriter
warning
wheel
window